# RYA
# Handy Guide to Marine Radio
## (inc. GMDSS)

**RYA**

The Royal Yachting Association
RYA House, Ensign Way,
Hamble, Southampton,
Hampshire SO31 4YA
Tel: 02380 604 100
Web: www.rya.org.uk

We welcome feedback on our publications at publications@rya.org.uk

You can check content updates for RYA publications at www.rya.org.uk/go/bookschangelog

ISBN 9781910017180
RYA Order Code G22

All rights reserved. No part of this publication may be reproduced, stored in a retrieval system, or transmitted, in any form or by any means, electronic, mechanical, photocopying, recording or otherwise, without the prior permission in writing of the publishers.

Published by the Royal Yachting Association
© 2017 Royal Yachting Association
Reprinted February 2019
Reprinted April 2021
Reprinted November 2021
Reprinted August 2022
Reprinted July 2023
Reprinted October 2024

Cover photographs: McMurdo, Standard Horizon
Cover design & typesetting: Jude Williams
Proofreading: Matthew Gale
Acknowledgement: Ian Waugh
Printed in the UK

# Contents

| | |
|---|---|
| Introduction | 4 |
| GMDSS | 5 |
| Radio Procedures | 9 |
| Installation & Maintenance | 20 |
| Licensing | 25 |
| Annexes | 28 |

# INTRODUCTION

Marine communications have been revolutionised by the introduction of the Global Maritime Distress and Safety System (GMDSS). Designed by the International Maritime Organisation and supported by the International Telecommunication Union, it ensures that ships anywhere in the world can communicate with an onshore rescue co-ordination centre by two independent means without the need for a specialist radio operator.

Pleasure vessels and Small Craft are not bound to carry radio transmitters and receivers, and are under no obligation to participate in the GMDSS. However, any sailor who wants to communicate with other ships, harbour authorities, and rescue co-ordination centres needs to keep up to date with the equipment and techniques of the commercial shipping world.

Some elements of pre-GMDSS communication will continue to be available but it will become increasingly important for sailors to participate in the GMDSS if they want to be certain of the ability to send a quick, effective Distress message.

Although in inshore waters mobile phones have proven to be effective, they are not a substitute for a marine VHF radio. They do not have the ability to participate in an open network, or receive and transmit broadcast messages such as Urgency and Safety messages. They can prove useful in emergencies when there is no marine VHF radio on board.

The continuing strength of maritime VHF is the facility to provide discrete ship-to-ship or ship-to-shore conversations and to broadcast messages.

With hundreds of thousands of users sharing fewer than 100 international channels there have to be rules and procedures which are understood and followed by everyone. They don't have to be followed slavishly but, if they were totally ignored, communication would be impossible.

The purpose of this book is to explain how boaters can join the international community of VHF marine radiotelephony, providing for their own safety without interfering with other users.

# GMDSS

During the 1970s, very large ships were built to transport cargo and, thanks to computer technology, marine VHF radios became smaller and easier for bridge watchkeepers to operate.

The International Maritime Organisation (IMO) became concerned that radio Distress messages were not always heard by other ships and, as a result, introduced the Global Maritime Distress and Safety System. This system requires that ships over 300 gross register tons, known as 'compulsory fit' vessels, are fitted with certain items of safety equipment and, most importantly, can send a digital and very audible alarm to others when they are in distress.

These vessels must carry:

- VHF Digital Selective Calling (DSC) marine radio (and MF/HF if in areas other than A1)
- 406MHz Emergency Position Indicating Radio Beacon (EPIRB) Radar
- Search and Rescue Radar Transponder (SART)
- Navtex
- Automatic Identification System (AIS)

Smaller vessels not covered by the GMDSS rules are referred to as 'voluntary fit vessels' but are strongly advised to fit DSC sets so that they can also summon help quickly and efficiently.

While large merchant ships are fitted with Class A or B DSC sets, leisure craft are usually fitted with the less-sophisticated and less-expensive Class D set.

DSC is simply a method of alerting another ship and subsequent voice communication is just as important as it was before the introduction of DSC.

# GMDSS

## GMDSS Areas

The world has been divided into four GMDSS areas and the radio equipment that vessels must carry depends on the sea areas in which they sail. The areas in NW Europe are shown below.

- **Sea area A1**
Within range of shorebased VHF coast stations fitted with DSC (30 to 50 miles, depending upon height of aerial and the power of the set).

- **Sea area A2**
Within range of shorebased MF/HF coast stations fitted with DSC (100 to 300 miles).

- **Sea area A3**
Within the coverage area of INMARSAT satellites (between roughly 70°N and 70°S).

- **Sea area A4**
The remaining sea areas using HF DSC.

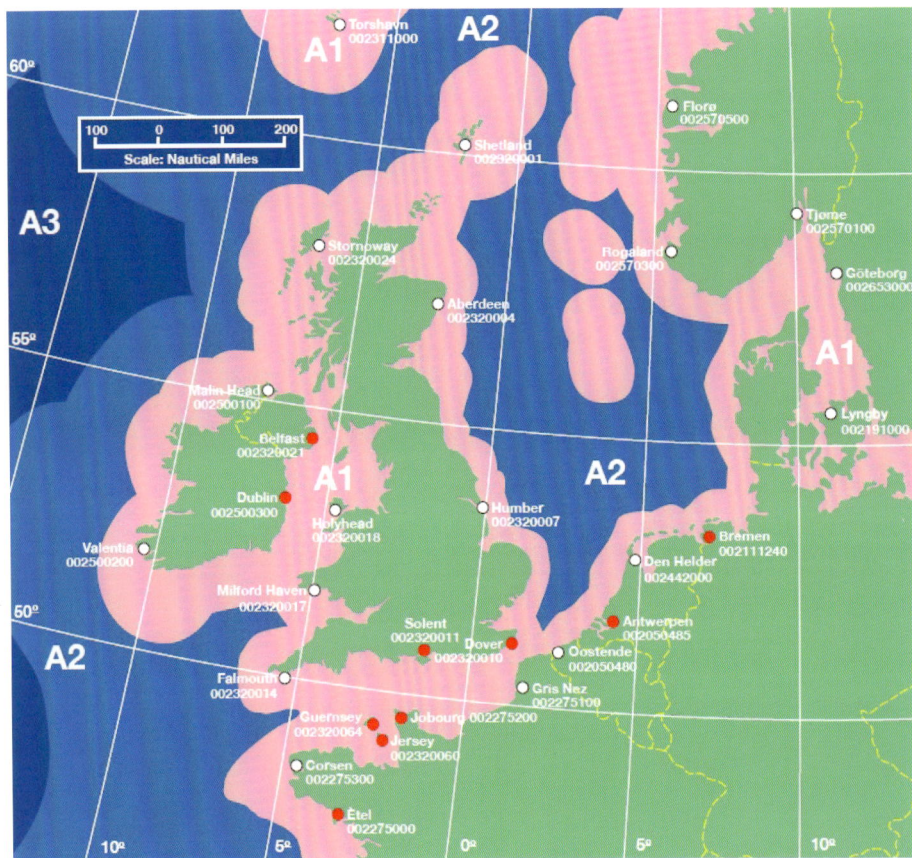

# GMDSS

## Navtex

Navtex is a component part of the GMDSS. Search & Rescue information together with navigational warnings, gale warnings and weather forecasts are sent at regular intervals from a series of transmitters positioned round the globe. All Navtex receivers use 518KHz, medium frequency, to receive information in English. More-advanced equipment is also fitted with 490KHz to receive additional information in the local language. In the UK, 490KHz is used for the Inshore Waters Forecast and the extended outlook. Depending on conditions, signals can be received at distances of up to 300 miles and the data can either be printed or shown on a digital display similar to the one shown below. The special antenna should be mounted clear of metal structures and well away from sources of electrical interference.

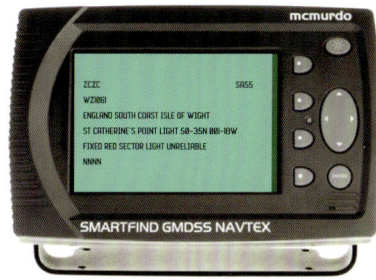 

**ZCZC**     The four characters ZCZC are used to begin every Navtex message.

**SA55**     This four-character code is usually the second item in any Navtex message. Each of the four characters has a meaning:

- The first character (S in this example) is the transmitter identity. It lets you know who the message is from. You can select which transmitters your Navtex receives messages from.

- The second letter (A in this example) is the subject indicator identifying the class of message and informing the user of what the message is about.

- The third and fourth characters (55 in this example) are the serial numbers of the message. They are allocated by the station the message comes from and will always be between 01 and 99.

**WZ1061**     WZ denotes this as a Maritime Safety Information (MSI) message. It is MSI message number 1061. This message would also be broadcast on VHF radio and include Whiskey Zulu 1061 before the message is broadcast.

**NNNN**     The four characters NNNN are used to signify that all of the message has been sent and that it is the end of the message.

### Navtex Message Categories

| | | | |
|---|---|---|---|
| **A*** | Navigational warnings | **K** | Other electronic navigational aids |
| **B*** | Meteorological warnings | **L** | SUBFACTS/GUNFACTS for the UK |
| **C** | Ice reports | **V** | Amplifying navigation warnings initially sent under A; plus weekly oil and gas rig moves |
| **D*** | Search & Rescue info and piracy attack warnings | | |
| **E** | Weather forecasts | **W–Y** | Special service – trial allocation |
| **F** | Pilot service | **Z** | No messages on hand at scheduled time |
| **G** | AIS messages | **I** and **M–U** are not at present allocated | |
| **H** | Loran-C | *These categories cannot be rejected by the receiver.* | |
| **J** | Satellite navigation | | |

# GMDSS

## Maritime Safety Information (MSI) Broadcasts

As soon as a Gale or Strong Wind warning is issued an announcement is made on Channel 16. This will direct listeners to a working channel, typically channels 62, 63, or 64. Routine weather-information broadcasts are made three-hourly, with a new forecast every six hours.

The full broadcast referred to in the table contains the Shipping Forecast; the new Inshore Waters forecast; the 24-hour outlook; Gale and Strong Wind warnings; navigational warnings; the fishers' three-day forecast, and SUBFACTS/GUNFACTS (where appropriate). Coastguard Operation Centres are indicated by CGOC; the National Maritime Operation Centre by NMOC.

| COASTGUARD | Three-hourly (local time) from | FULL BROADCAST | INSHORE WATERS AREAS |
|---|---|---|---|
| Aberdeen CGOC | 0130 | 0730 & 1930 | Cape Wrath to Rattray Head inc. Orkney. Rattray Head to Berwick-upon-Tweed. |
| Humber CGOC | 0150 | 0750 & 1950 | Berwick-upon-Tweed to Whitby. Whitby to Gibraltar Point. Gibraltar Point to North Foreland. |
| Dover CGOC | 0110 | 0710 & 1910 | Gibraltar Point to North Foreland. North Foreland to Selsey Bill. |
| Fareham NMOC (Solent CGOC) | 0130 | 0730 & 1930 | North Foreland to Selsey Bill. Selsey Bill to Lyme Regis. Lyme Regis to Land's End. |
| Falmouth CGOC | 0110 | 0710 & 1910 | Lyme Regis to Land's End inc. Isles of Scilly. Land's End to St David's Head. |
| Milford Haven CGOC | 0150 | 0750 & 1950 | Land's End to St David's Head inc. Bristol Channel. St David's Head to Great Orme Head, including St George's Channel. |
| Holyhead CGOC | 0130 | 0730 & 1930 | St David's Head to Great Orme Head, including St George's Channel. Isle of Man. Great Orme Head to the Mull of Galloway. |
| Belfast CGOC | 0210 | 0810 & 2010 | Mull of Galloway to Mull of Kintyre inc. Firth of Clyde and North Channel. Carlingford Lough to Lough Foyle. Mull of Kintyre to Ardnamurchan. |
| Stornoway SGOC | 0110 | 0710 & 1910 | Mull of Kintyre to Ardnamurchan. The Minch. Ardnamurchan to Cape Wrath. |
| Shetland | 0110 | 0710 & 1910 | Shetland Isles within 60 miles of Lerwick. Cape Wrath to Rattray Head inc. Orkney. |

*Correct at time of publication.*

Details of European shore stations issuing meteorological bulletins at fixed times are published in nautical almanacs.

# RADIO PROCEDURES

## Using the Radio

English was chosen as the international radio language over 100 years ago. Radio channels should never be used for social chatter. All conversations – called 'traffic' – should be about the safety or the manoeuvring of a boat so that vital Distress and Urgency messages are not missed. The mobile phone should be used to discuss football scores or the local restaurant's menu!

## The Radio Regulations

The International Telecommunication Union gives the following list of 'strictly forbidden transmissions' so that interference is not caused to others.

1. The transmission of profane, indecent or obscene language.
2. Making unnecessary transmissions or transmitting superfluous signals. (This includes whistling into the microphone or discussing the football results!)
3. Transmissions made without identification – the boat's name must be stated every time the microphone is keyed.
4. The broadcast of music.
5. The transmission of false or deceptive Distress, Safety or identification signals.
6. Transmissions not authorised by the skipper or person in charge of the boat.
7. Operation of the radio by an unauthorised person. Passengers or other members of the crew may make radio telephone calls under the supervision of a qualified operator.
8. The broadcast of messages to an unlicensed shore station. If you have a VHF scanner at home you may not broadcast to your partner that you will be home for tea at 1600!
9. The use of personal names or unauthorised names in lieu of the boat's name.
10. Closing down the radio before finishing all operations resulting from a Distress call. If you have been involved in the rescue of a casualty you must not shut the radio down until the Coastguard stands you down.
11. The use of frequencies or channels other than those covered by the ship's licence.

## Secrecy of Correspondence

Anyone who becomes acquainted with the content of radio telephone calls is legally bound to preserve the secrecy of correspondence and not 'improperly divulge' the contents or even the existence of correspondence transmitted, received or intercepted.

## Getting Ready to Make a Routine Call (without DSC)

1. Turn the set on and adjust the squelch.
2. Adjust the volume and select Low Power.
3. Select Channel 16.
4. Before transmitting, check that other people are not using the chosen channel. If it is occupied, wait for the end of the conversation or find another channel.
5. Hold the microphone about eight centimetres from the mouth then press the switch on the microphone to transmit. Do not speak until you have pressed the button.
6. Prepare to speak clearly and slowly at a normal conversation level. If somebody is likely to write your message, slow down even more.
7. Try to avoid dropping the voice at the end of a word or phrase. If you have a strong accent, try to make your pronunciation as clear as possible.

# RADIO PROCEDURES

## How to Call

First, you must decide how many times you are going to call the other station's name. The general rule is:

### Calling another Ship Station

1. Say their name twice if they are likely to be near the radio but if the weather is bad and the wind is howling it may be prudent to call three times. The rules state that the maximum is three times.
2. Say your name twice or three times as necessary.

Example call on Channel 16:

*Seaspray, Seaspray, this is Blue Dolphin, Blue Dolphin. Suggest channel zero eight. Over.*
*Answer: Blue Dolphin, this is Seaspray. Switching to channel zero eight.*

Both boats allow time for switching channels, then Seaspray makes the first call on Channel 8:

*Blue Dolphin, this is Seaspray on Channel 8. Over.*

*Answer: Seaspray, Blue Dolphin. Pass your message. Over.*

### Control of Communication

Officially it is the station being called who controls communication. However, when DSC is being used it is the caller who chooses the channel. Of course, the called station may always change the channel if it thinks it necessary.

When DSC is not used it is still preferable for the caller to offer a known empty channel so that the time spent talking on Channel 16 is reduced to a minimum. In all cases a Coast Station controls communication.

### Calling a Marina

1. Select the working channel of the marina (normally Channel 80 in the UK) then say their name just once as they are usually listening for calls.

2. Say your own ship's name twice.

Example:

*Mercury Marina this is Motor Yacht Blue Dolphin, Blue Dolphin. Over.*
*Answer: Blue Dolphin, this is Mercury. What can I do for you? Over.*
*Mercury, Blue Dolphin, request a berth for one night for a twelve-metre motor yacht. Over.*

### Unanswered Calls

If you have made a routine call to another ship station and receive no reply, check that the volume and the squelch control are set correctly and that you are tuned to an appropriate channel. Turn to High Power.

In any event, you must wait for at least two minutes before calling again. You are permitted to call three times at two-minute intervals, after which you must wait three minutes before trying again.

As a rule, if another boat has not answered you after two calls they are probably not listening – do not call again.

# RADIO PROCEDURES

## Position

When latitude and longitude are used these shall be expressed in degrees and minutes (and decimals of a minute if necessary) north or south of the equator and east or west of Greenwich.

The numerals should be spoken digit by digit.

Example: **50° 12′.4N 001° 27′.7W** should be read:

***Five zero degrees one two decimal four minutes north, zero zero one degrees two seven decimal seven minutes west.***

When the position is related to a mark, it should be a well-defined charted object. The bearing should be in the 360° notation from True North and be that of the position FROM the mark.

Example:
*My position is one eight zero degrees from Portland Bill Lighthouse two decimal four miles.*

## Distances

Distances are preferably to be expressed in nautical miles or cables (tenths of a mile). Metres and kilometres may be used but the unit used should always be stated.

## Speed

Speed is to be expressed in knots. There should be no further notation meaning speed through the water.

## Time

Use the 24-hour clock and indicate whether it is UTC (Universal Time), local time or zone time.

## Garbled Calls

When a station receives a call but is uncertain for whom it is intended (Example: …this is Born Free – over) it must not reply until the call has been repeated and understood.

## Unknown Calling Station

When a station receives a call intended for it but is uncertain of the name of the calling station, it should reply:

*Station calling Barbican – This is Barbican – say again – over.*

## Use of the Radiotelephone when in Port

Generally a radiotelephone may be used only for port operations and on private channels (e.g. Channel M2) when in UK harbours and estuaries. Use the mobile phone to talk to another boat in the marina – not the VHF radio.

## DSC Alerts & Calls

In the radio regulations, Distress alerts sent by Digital Selective Calling are the only true alerts. All other DSC transmissions are referred to as Urgency, Safety, or routine DSC calls. In this book, we refer to all DSC transmissions as alerts to avoid confusion between a DSC Urgency call and a subsequent Urgency call (by voice).

# RADIO PROCEDURES

## Urgency, Safety & Coastguard Liaison

### Urgency Messages

The general Urgency messages are prefixed with the words Pan-Pan repeated three times. This indicates that the vessel or crew have a serious problem but are not in a Distress situation.

It is often difficult to decide whether to send a Mayday or Pan-Pan message. Consider the definition of Distress: 'Grave and imminent danger and requires immediate assistance'. Anything less may justify an Urgency signal.

Examples of Urgency include a boat taking on water, but not yet sinking; an engine failure with no other means of propulsion but some distance from a lee shore, and injury to a crew member who needs treatment but whose life is not threatened. Remember that an Urgency situation can always be upgraded to a Distress one.

### Urgency alerting by DSC

Using DSC, select 'Urgency Call' and press the Enter button.

The equipment will ask for confirmation that an Urgency call is required.

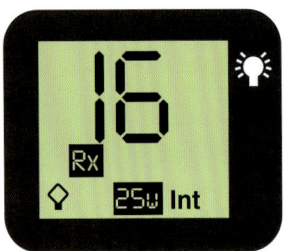

Once it has got the confirmation it will then send the alert and the radio will automatically switch to Channel 16.

On receipt by an operator in another vessel, the audio alarm will sound and the VHF radio will automatically switch to Channel 16.

The visual display will indicate that an Urgency call has been received and will display the MMSI of the issuing ship station. Unlike Distress, Urgency alerts do not include the ship's position (even though this may be displayed on the sender's screen) so it is essential that this is included in the voice Urgency message.

12  RYA Handy Guide to Marine Radio (inc. GMDSS)

# RADIO PROCEDURES

## The Urgency Call and Message

After sending the DSC alert the operator must wait 15 seconds before sending the voice Urgency call and message on Channel 16. Whether DSC is fitted or not, the voice message is almost identical; the only difference is that the MMSI must be given if DSC is present.

It will be seen from the examples below that the message by voice should be addressed to a particular station or stations. This could be to 'All ships', 'All stations' or to a local HM Coastguard Station. Note that if an Urgency alert has been sent by DSC then the vessel's MMSI must be included in the Urgency message to enable the alert and the message to be correlated.

**Pan-Pan, Pan-Pan, Pan-Pan**
**All stations, all stations, all stations**

**This is** (Name three times and call sign)

**MMSI**
**Position** (either latitude and longitude or bearing and distance FROM a charted object)
**Nature of urgency**
**Assistance required**
**Number of persons on board**
**Other useful information to assist**
**Over**

An example of such a message is as follows:

**Pan-Pan, Pan-Pan, Pan-Pan**
**Falmouth Coastguard, Falmouth Coastguard, Falmouth Coastguard**

**This is Motor Yacht Unfortunate, Unfortunate, Unfortunate**

**Call sign MCFX9 MMSI 234001546**

**My position is 49° 38'.45N 006° 20'.14W**
**Total engine failure and drifting**
**I require assistance to clear Traffic Separation Scheme**
**Two persons on board**
**Colour of hull black, upperwork white**
**Over**

The nearest Coast Station will normally acknowledge a DSC Urgency alert and message by voice, provided that it is in VHF range. The Coastguard may also repeat the Pan-Pan message on Channel 16, after which they will take control of further traffic.

There is no official structure for an Urgency message, but the above example can be taken as a suggested one.

## Safety

The proword for Safety messages is 'Sécurité', pronounced 'say-cure-ee-tay'. This word is spoken three times, indicating that the station is about to transmit a message containing an important navigational or meteorological warning. It normally originates from a shore authority but may, under special circumstances, be sent by a vessel at sea. This will be a rare event and only likely if you were to sight something like a partially submerged container in an area of high-density traffic.

# RADIO PROCEDURES

### The DSC Safety Alert

Select 'Safety Call' from the call menu. Now press the 'Enter' button. The equipment will ask for confirmation that you wish to send a Safety alert (below) and, when confirmed, will send the alert. Your VHF radio will automatically switch to Channel 16. Some equipment allows you to select a working channel.

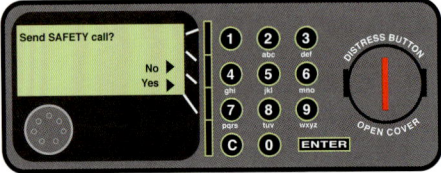

The Safety alert is less strident than Distress and Urgency. It will be heard on a receiving vessel and by the Coastguard, their visual displays indicating that a Safety alert has been received. Receiving stations should be prepared to write down any subsequent message.

### The Safety Call

A Safety call, given by voice on Channel 16, will announce which working channel is to be used for the main body of the message.

Example on Channel 16:

*Sécurité, Sécurité, Sécurité*
*All stations, all stations, all stations*
*This is Humber Coastguard, Humber Coastguard, Humber Coastguard*
*For urgent navigational warning listen Channel 67*
*Out*

Then on Channel 67:

*Sécurité, Sécurité, Sécurité*
*All stations, all stations, all stations*
*This is Humber Coastguard, Humber Coastguard, Humber Coastguard*
*Large drifting hulk reported in position five one degrees four zero minutes North,*
*one degree one zero minutes East*
*Considered to be a danger to surface navigation*
*Time of origin one two three zero UTC*
*Out*

All stations hearing the Safety call on Channel 16 should switch to the working channel (Channel 67). They must listen to the message until they are satisfied that it is of no concern to them. They must not make any transmission likely to interfere with the message.

## Distress Procedures

### Definition of Distress

The definition of distress in the 1979 Search and Rescue Convention is:
*Grave and Imminent Danger to a Person, Ship, Aircraft or Other Vehicle Requiring Immediate Assistance.*

Distress is announced using the word 'Mayday', derived from the French 'M'aidez', meaning 'Help me'. This prefix must only be used for Distress traffic and, except in a Distress situation, the word 'Mayday' should never be used on the radio even in conversation.

# RADIO PROCEDURES

Emergencies that do not fall into the distress category but where an urgent message needs to be passed concerning the safety of a person, ship, aircraft or other vehicle, are Urgency messages prefixed 'Pan-Pan'. Transmissions concerning the safety of navigation are prefixed 'Sécurité'. Urgency and Safety are covered on pages 12–13.

## Distress Transmission

There are three separate parts to a Distress transmission:

A. The DSC Distress alert
B. The voice Distress call
C. The voice Distress message

Parts A, B and C are used if DSC is fitted; parts B and C if it is not.

### To Send a Distress Alert

The illustration to the left shows the display after one press of the RED button and selection of the nature of distress.

To send an undesignated Distress alert from the DSC you should:

1. Lift the cover of the RED Distress button
2. Press the RED Distress button for five seconds
3. The equipment will now automatically send an electronic data burst on Channel 70 giving:

   a) your MMSI

   b) your position (from GPS or manual entry)

   c) the time the Distress alert was sent

   d) the nature of distress (if selected)

4. The screen will indicate Channel 16 – it is automatically tuned in preparation for voice communication.
5. The VHF DSC apparatus will repeat the Distress alert approximately every four minutes until a digital acknowledgement is received.
6. Wait 15 seconds and then give the voice Distress call and message on Channel 16.

If time permits, the radio's menu system can allow you to set a specific designation for the type of distress, such as fire or sinking.

RYA Handy Guide to Marine Radio (inc. GMDSS)   15

# RADIO PROCEDURES

### The Distress Call

A Distress call has absolute priority over all other transmissions. All stations hearing it must immediately cease any transmissions which could cause interference to the Distress traffic. They must then continue to listen on the frequency for the Distress message.

*Mayday, Mayday, Mayday*
*This is yacht Calamity, Calamity, Calamity,* Call sign and MMSI (if DSC is fitted)

### The Distress Message

The Distress message follows the Distress call without a break and should be spoken slowly and clearly. Remember that your rescuer will be trying to write down your position and other details. The internationally recognised format is:

**Mayday Yacht Calamity**
**Call sign and MMSI**
**Position** (in latitude and longitude or a true bearing and distance from a prominent charted object)
**Nature of distress** (fire, sinking, hit a submerged object etc.)
**Assistance required**
**Other useful information** (anything that may assist the rescuer e.g. total number of persons on board as it could affect the choice of rescue method, taking to liferaft, person injured etc.)
**Over** (awaiting a reply)

The following is an example of a complete voice Distress transmission following a DSC Distress alert:

**Mayday, Mayday, Mayday**
**This is Yacht Calamity, Calamity, Calamity, call sign ZZBA, MMSI 234001234**
**Mayday Yacht Calamity call sign ZZBA, MMSI 234001234**
**My position is 50° 46'N 001° 17'W**
**Swamped in rough sea and sinking**
**I require immediate assistance**
**Five people on board**
**Abandoning to liferaft**
**Over**

### Emergency Procedure Cards

It is strongly recommended that an emergency procedure card is affixed to a bulkhead close to the radio set. Copies of suitable cards are shown on pages 32 and 33.

# RADIO PROCEDURES

## Receiving a Distress Message

The International Regulations state, 'The obligation to accept Distress calls and messages is absolute in the case of every station without distinction, and such messages must be accepted with priority over all other messages, they must be answered and the necessary steps must immediately be taken to give effect to them.'

Class D equipment does not enable you to acknowledge a Mayday digitally or to switch off the DSC alerting system in another craft; that requires a Coast Station or a vessel fitted with a Class A or B controller. It is likely that a Coast Station will accept responsibility for the rescue within a very short time and is in an ideal position to help with lifeboats, helicopters and medical aid. If you hear a Distress alert and message you should:

1. Write down all the distress information and inform your skipper
2. Wait for a Coast Station acknowledgement

It is likely that a coast radio station (such as the Coastguard) will have received the message – allow them up to five minutes to respond before doing so yourself. If you have not heard anything from the Coastguard or other vessels within five minutes, acknowledge the alert by voice on Channel 16. You should then attempt to relay the distress message to a coast station using any available means, usually by voice Mayday Relay call and message.

The voice format of a Coastguard response will be:

**Mayday Yacht Calamity, call sign ZZBA (or MMSI)**
**This is Solent Coastguard**
**Received Mayday**
**Standby**

## Mayday Relay Procedure

A ship or shore station that learns of a vessel in distress should transmit a Mayday Relay call and message when:

1. The station in distress cannot itself transmit a Distress message
2. Sighting a non-radio Distress signal (flares, fire, flags or shapes)
3. Although not in a position to render assistance, she has heard a Distress message which has not been acknowledged within five minutes

When a station, not herself in distress, is transmitting a Mayday Relay this fact must be made quite clear. If this is not done, direction-finding bearings might be taken on the station transmitting the relay and assistance could be directed to the wrong position.

## Using DSC to Send a Mayday Relay

The Class D VHF DSC has no facility for sending a Distress Relay alert, so a Mayday Relay should be sent by voice only.

# RADIO PROCEDURES

## The Mayday Relay Call and Message

The Mayday Relay call and message are formatted as follows:

**Mayday Relay** (x3)

**Specific Coastguard station** (x3) **or** *all stations* (x3)

**This is** (name (x3) and call sign and MMSI of the station making the transmission)

**Mayday** (Name of vessel in distress and call sign and MMSI, if known)

**Position of vessel in distress**

**Nature of the distress**

**Assistance required**

**Other information** (e.g. number of people on board, the time received)

**Over**

For example, Motor Yacht Bluebell has heard a Mayday message from the Yacht Calamity. No one has acknowledged after five minutes. Bluebell sends a Mayday Relay call targeted to a Coastguard station and a repeat of the mayday message:

*Mayday Relay, Mayday Relay, Mayday Relay*

*Solent Coastguard, Solent Coastguard, Solent Coastguard*

*This is Motor Yacht Bluebell, Bluebell, Bluebell, call sign ZZWX, MMSI 233000285*
*Mayday Yacht Calamity, call sign ZZBA, MMSI 234001526*
*Position 50° 46'N 001° 17'W*
*Swamped in rough sea and sinking*
*Require immediate assistance*
*Five persons on board*
*Abandoning to liferaft*
*Over*

## Imposing Radio Silence

The station controlling Distress traffic may impose silence. To achieve this it transmits:

*Mayday*

*All stations, all stations, all stations*

*This is Solent Coastguard, Solent Coastguard, Solent Coastguard*

*Seelonce Mayday*

*Out*

# RADIO PROCEDURES

### Cancelling Radio Silence

When the Distress traffic has completely ceased, the station which has controlled the Distress traffic must let all stations know that normal working may be resumed. This is done using the expression 'Seelonce Feenee'. For example:

*Mayday*

*All stations, all stations, all stations*

*This is Dover Coastguard, Dover Coastguard, Dover Coastguard*

*Time 1045 UTC*

*Yacht Calamity*

*Seelonce Feenee*

*Out*

## False Alerts

Much time and money can be expended searching for a distressed vessel after a false alert. It is essential that the procedure for cancelling a false alert is known and used immediately when the mistake is realised.

## False VHF DSC Distress Alert

Allow the alert transmission to complete once. If no acknowledgement is received from another station, switch off the DSC equipment to prevent a repeat transmission. Switch VHF equipment back on and set to Channel 16. Make an 'All Stations' voice broadcast giving ship's name, MMSI and position. Cancel False Distress and give time. Example:

*All stations, all stations, all stations*

*This is Yacht Dunce, Dunce, Dunce, Mike, Yankee, Foxtrot, Tango, Seven, MMSI 233003765*

*Cancel Distress alert sent at 0245 UTC*

*Out*

### 406MHz False EPIRB Alert

Switch off the 406 EPIRB beacon. Report the false alert to the nearest Coastguard by any means, relaying through another station if necessary.

# INSTALLATION & MAINTENANCE

## Marine VHF & Digital Selective Calling Equipment

### Fitting VHF

#### Position

The radiotelephone is usually located in the cabin of a small boat. It should be:

- securely fastened
- in a convenient position clear of spray and dampness
- away from the engine and any heat source

The set is connected to the yacht's power supply (observing the correct polarity) with the antenna feeder cable connected. No earth is needed. A waterproof extension loudspeaker, sited close to the steering position, allows the helm to monitor the radio and some sets allow the Distress button to be pressed from the helm position.

#### Power Supplies

While receiving, the radio consumes very little current. While transmitting, the current may rise to five or more amps. Generally, transmissions are infrequent and unlikely to present a serious drain on the boat's battery. It is good practice to have a battery specifically for communications that can be isolated from the main circuit. However, it would be prudent to carry a hand-held radio in case the boat's battery becomes waterlogged.

#### Antennas

- The High Gain Antenna is about two metres long and concentrates the radiated power along a narrow horizontal beam, giving greater ranges if the antenna is kept nearly vertical, as on a motor cruiser.

- The Unity Gain Antenna, about one metre long, has a radiated beam with a wider spread. As it's less likely to be affected by heeling it is recommended for sailing yachts.

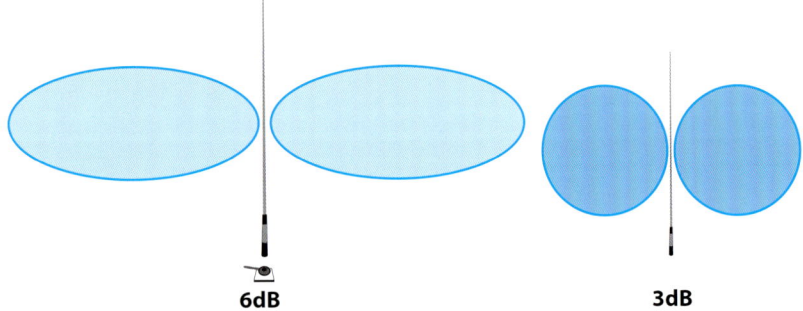

6dB    3dB

Ideally, the full power available from the transmitter should be radiated from the antenna but there will always be some loss in the feeder cable. Use the best-quality low-loss cable from the radiotelephone to the antenna and keep the number of connectors or joins to a minimum.

# INSTALLATION & MAINTENANCE

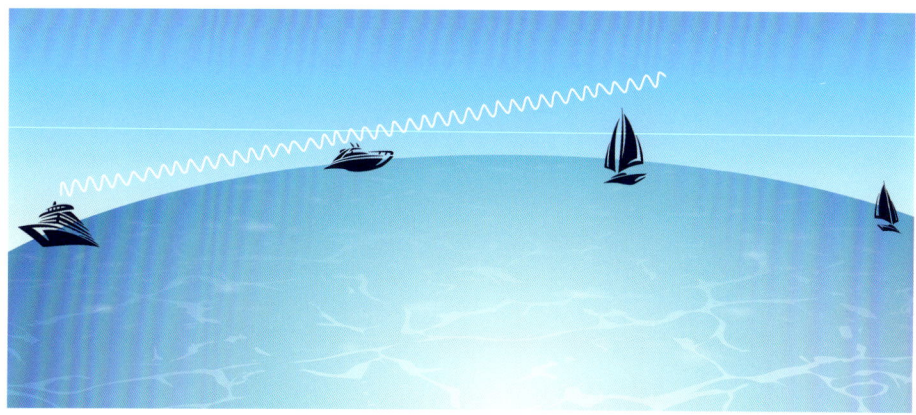

The propagation of VHF radio waves is little more than line-of-sight, so antenna height is very important. It's normally positioned at the masthead as any lower down it may be masked by the rigging, making communication difficult on certain relative bearings. A secondary, portable hand-held antenna will be invaluable in an emergency. Longer-range radio communications using medium frequency and high frequency use a different method of propagation to achieve their greater range. The following illustrations show this but are not relevant to VHF communication.

Medium-frequency transmissions are able to follow the curvature of the earth, and have a greater range than the 'line-of-sight' VHF waves.

# INSTALLATION & MAINTENANCE

High-frequency transmissions are bounced off the ionosphere and back down to earth. They have the greatest range of all.

Care should be taken to avoid running the antenna feeder cable near other cables feeding sensitive equipment such as wind instruments, logs and electronic self-steering equipment – even low-loss cable will radiate.

Radio waves can be affected by various factors. High barometric pressure or increased humidity often give greater ranges than normal. Rough seas, causing the ship's antenna to sway back and forth, will cause disruption and reduce the range considerably.

## Emergency Radio Equipment

### Emergency Position Indicating Radio Beacons (EPIRBs)

An EPIRB is portable, battery-operated, waterproof and buoyant. It transmits a Distress alert and allows Search and Rescue (SAR) organisations to pinpoint the position of survivors.

# INSTALLATION & MAINTENANCE

For all practical purposes there are two types of EPIRB available to boat owners, both of which use the COSPAS-SARSAT satellite system. They work on the 406MHz and 121.5MHz bands, and are applicable to all sea areas, although the 121.5MHz personal locator beacons are outside the scope of this book.

### 406MHz with 121.5MHz

The 406 (pictured right) is useful to anyone venturing offshore. The Search and Rescue satellites listen to and store the emergency message until they are over a ground station, making it possible to provide worldwide coverage. The 406 also has an embedded code which contains the vessel's identification number. The precision and power of the transmitted signal, which includes 121.5MHz as a homing device, allows the satellite to calculate the position of the beacon to within a two-mile radius.

### 406MHz with GPS

A 406MHz EPIRB (pictured right) has been designed with an integral miniature GPS which transmits current position and further enhances its lifesaving capabilities. When the beacon is activated, this positional information is incorporated into the Distress message it transmits. GPS EPIRBs can fix the position to within 25 metres, a great improvement in accuracy.

Careful thought must be given to the installation of the EPIRB. It may be on deck attached by hydrostatic release or stored in a grab bag. In either case it must be protected from accidental release and inquisitive fingers. If it is accidentally activated you must inform the nearest Coastguard as soon as possible, giving details of the beacon and switching it off. This must not be done until the rescue authorities have been contacted, otherwise a search may continue for many hours to locate the source of the transmission.

When an EPIRB is purchased it must be added to the Ship Radio licence and registered with the EPIRB registry in your particular country. This is a legal requirement.

# INSTALLATION & MAINTENANCE

## Search and Rescue Transponder (SART)

The SART is a small battery-operated distress beacon (right) that responds to a radar beam from a potential rescuer. It should be deployed as high as possible and, once activated, a surface craft's radar should pick up the signal from about five miles, and a helicopter at 3000ft from about 30 miles. This signal is displayed initially as a series of dots on the bearing of the casualty and later as concentric circles covering the display as shown below. If the SART is activated by accident you must inform the Coastguard without delay in case a passing ship thinks that a Distress situation exists.

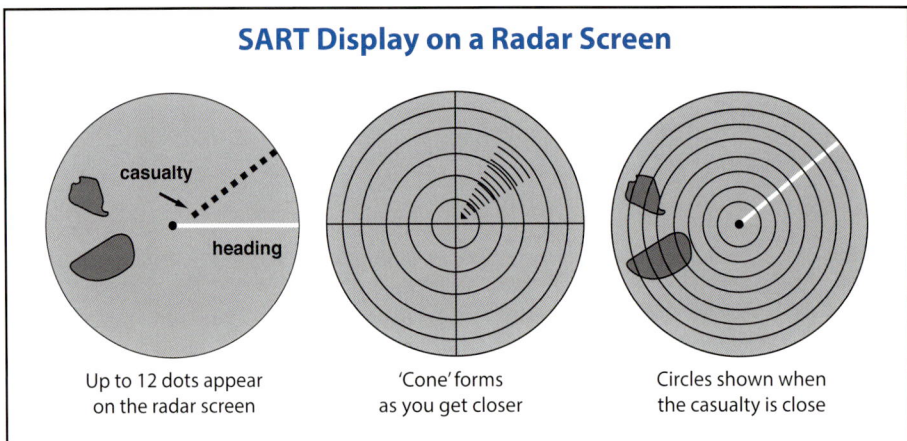

### SART Display on a Radar Screen

Up to 12 dots appear on the radar screen

'Cone' forms as you get closer

Circles shown when the casualty is close

## AIS SART

The Automatic Identification System Search and Rescue Transmitter is a radio device that derives position from a GPS receiver. When activated, once per minute the AIS SART sends its position via two VHF channels.

# LICENSING

## The Requirement

When fitting a VHF radiotelephone, the owner of any vessel must make sure that they satisfy three requirements:

1. The equipment being fitted must be 'type approved'

2. The equipment must be licensed

3. The operator must be qualified or be under the direct supervision of someone who holds an operator's certificate

## Type Approval

Marine radio equipment offered for sale in the UK must conform to the technical requirements of the Radio Equipment Directive (RED) and should carry an identification mark similar to the one shown below.

The general principle of the directive is that radio equipment has to do its job without being dangerous and without causing unnecessary interference, but the test requirement has gone. The manufacturer now has to issue a declaration of conformity, formally certifying that the radio conforms to the appropriate performance standards, and ensure that it is marked with the familiar CE label.

Second-hand sets or those bought overseas may not be fitted with the correct channels and often do not conform to the European standard. Such sets could be confiscated by Office of Communications (Ofcom) staff as they carry out their routine inspections.

The Ofcom website has information on all the radio regulations. If you have any doubts about your own equipment consult Ofcom on www.ofcom.org.uk or telephone them on 020 7981 3000.

The Royal Yachting Association and the Maritime & Coastguard Agency (MCA) are always willing to assist with questions on procedure and may be contacted as follows:

RYA: www.rya.org.uk

MCA: 0203 817 2000

## The Ship Radio Licence

The Wireless Telegraphy Act of 1949 requires that all vessels fitted with radio equipment have a valid Ship Radio Licence. This licence is valid for the lifetime of the vessel but owners are required to renew it every 10 years or if equipment is changed. It is free of charge if the initial application and renewal is completed online using the Ofcom website, but postal applications carry a charge of £20.

When first applying for a licence the applicant will be invited to open a user account and will be sent a password for any future communications. Ofcom will advise the owner about renewal after 10 years. It is important that the licence is carried on board the boat, especially when taking the boat out of UK waters to where the inspection procedures are more rigorous than those in the UK.

# LICENSING

The ship's licence covers all items that transmit, provided that they have been declared on the application form. It covers any or all of the following:

1. MF, HF or VHF radiotelephone equipment
2. Digital selective calling (DSC) equipment associated with the GMDSS
3. Hand-held marine VHF radios used on the parent craft or in the tender
4. Radar, and Search and Rescue Transponders (SARTs)
5. Emergency Position Indicating Radio Beacons (EPIRBs) using 406MHz or 121.5MHz
6. Satellite communications equipment (Ship Earth Stations)
7. Low-power on-board communications including UHF and repeater stations
8. AIS

Upon the original application, boats will be issued with a unique international call sign, which remains with the vessel through both change of ownership and equipment. A typical call sign would be MZD8T. DSC equipment will also be issued with a nine-figure identifying number called a Maritime Mobile Service Identity, or MMSI for short. MMSIs are discussed on page 27.

## Ship Portable Licence

A hand-held VHF radio which is intended for use in a variety of craft is required to have a Ship Portable Licence, which is free online and £20 by post. This set will be issued with an international call sign which includes the letter 'T' to denote that it is 'transportable' and licensed to an individual and not a vessel.

A hand-held VHF which includes DSC and GPS will be registered to an individual and allocated an MMSI beginning with the numbers 2359.

## Licences for Radios used by Yacht Clubs

In the UK, licences are available which permit yacht clubs and similar organisations to establish a base station. Full details are given in the Coastal Station Radio information booklet available from the Ofcom website (ofcom.org.uk) or from: Ofcom, Riverside House, 2a Southwark Bridge Road, London SE1 9HA. Telephone: 0207 981 3000.

## Operator Qualifications

To maintain operational standards and ensure a working knowledge of Distress, emergency and safety procedures, a maritime radio can only be operated by a holder of the appropriate operator's certificate or by someone under their direct personal supervision.

The MCA has contracted the RYA to conduct examinations and issue certificates for the Marine Radio Short Range Certificate (SRC). For anyone venturing much further offshore, the AMERC Organisation runs a similar scheme for the Long Range Certificate (see www.amerc.ac.uk).

The MCA is responsible to the European Telecommunications Union (CEPT) for operator standards within the United Kingdom and Northern Ireland. CEPT member states will accept the validity of UK certificates for use on British-registered craft but it would be wise to seek advice from the MCA when operating in foreign-flagged vessels.

The Marine Radio Short Range Certificate can only be issued following successful completion of an SRC exam conducted by an authorised SRC Assessor at a training centre recognised by the RYA for Marine Radio training and assessment. The exam consists of a theoretical test and practical assessment using VHF/DSC radios adapted for training purposes.

# LICENSING

To be eligible for the SRC exam, candidates must:

1. Be at least 16 years old on the day of the exam. Young persons under the age of 16 are welcome to attend an SRC course and will be awarded a course completion certificate/declaration but will not be eligible to take the exam until they are 16 years old.

2. Have completed an approved training course at an RYA Recognised Training Centre. This is typically the Marine Radio Short Range course delivered in the classroom over one day, or online via RYA Interactive. Candidates who hold the older Restricted VHF Certificate of Competence or other non-marine GMDSS licences may be eligible for assessment without attending the full course. These candidates should contact an RYA Recognised Training Centre to discuss their options and access suitable training and/or training material prior to the exam.

## Holders of Non-DSC VHF Operator's Certificates

Holders of the Restricted Certificate of Competence (VHF only), which was issued prior to the introduction of the SRC, may continue to operate non-DSC radios but must have knowledge of the Global Maritime Distress and Safety Scheme. If they intend to operate DSC equipment they must qualify for the SRC at an RYA Training Centre either by attending a course or by direct examination.

## RYA Training Centres

Further details about marine radio, including a list of suitable RYA Recognised Training Centres, are available from the RYA website: www.rya.org.uk/training/courses/marine-radio-short-range-certificate-course-srcc.

## Maritime Mobile Service Identity (MMSI)

An MMSI is a unique nine-digit number that identifies a particular ship or shore station, but can also identify groups of vessels, search-and-rescue aircraft, or navigation aids. Those for ship stations are issued free of charge by the licensing authority and entered into the set on purchase. Each MMSI contains the country code, UK vessels being identified with the numbers 232, 233, 234 or 235, US vessels by 338, 366, 367, 368 or 369, and Australian ones by 503. Individual vessels' MMSI numbers begin with the three-digit country code, followed by six digits identifying the craft.

Coast stations concerned with rescue co-ordination are identified with an MMSI beginning with two zeros. For example, Humber Coastguard's MMSI is 002320007. Important MMSIs are often listed in nautical almanacs and a searchable list of ship stations is kept by the ITU on their website: https://www.itu.int/mmsapp/ShipStation/list. If the vessel you wish to call is not listed you will need to obtain the MMSI from the boat owner.

# ANNEXES

## Simplex and Duplex Working

With simplex (found in most leisure craft and small workboats), transmission is only possible in one direction at a time; you can either transmit or receive but not simultaneously. The single antenna is switched from receive to transmit (and back again) by using the Press-to-transmit switch.

Duplex transmissions make it possible to transmit and receive simultaneously. It needs two frequencies and usually two antennas or a special duplex filter.

Ship-to-shore working channels are allocated on a two-frequency basis. For example, Channel 26 has two frequencies – the ship transmits on a frequency of 157.3MHz and the shore station transmits on 161.9MHz.

It is possible to use simplex equipment on the two frequency channels, but transmission is still only possible in one direction at a time. The Press-to-transmit switch automatically selects the correct frequency for transmission or reception.

## International Channels

Each channel is allocated for one or more of eight specific purposes and it is important to select a suitable channel for your particular use.

### Distress, Safety and Calling

Channel 16 has always been the VHF Distress Safety and Calling frequency and will remain so for the foreseeable future. The normal routine is to establish contact on Channel 16 and arrange to move to a mutually acceptable working frequency as quickly as possible.

However, with the number of radio telephones in use, in the busiest areas there is great pressure on Channel 16 and rescue centres fear that a Distress call may be missed due to congestion. Although all vessels are urged to maintain a continuous watch on Channel 16 when at sea, callers are encouraged to use working frequencies for initial calls whenever possible; this can only be done if the station called is maintaining a listening watch on that frequency.

Digital Selective Calling reduces congestion on Channel 16 as the initial electronic alert is sent as a very short data burst using Channel 70. Channel 70 must never be used for voice communication.

### Bridge-to-bridge

Channel 13 is an inter-ship channel reserved exclusively for bridge-to-bridge communication on matters of navigational safety.

### Inter-ship

Channels 6, 8, 72 and 77 should be used for inter-ship working because they are exclusively for that purpose. Other inter-ship channels are allocated for additional purposes; for example Channel 10 for pollution control and Channel 9 for harbour pilots (see page 34). Small Craft should avoid using these channels.

### Port Operations

Channels 11, 12 and 14 are most commonly used for port operations, but refer to a nautical almanac for local variations.

### Ship Movements

This is very similar to port operations. Ship movements are often conducted on the single-frequency channels such as Channels 15, 17 and 69.

# ANNEXES

## UK Small Craft Safety

Channel 67 is single-frequency ship-to-ship and is used by HM Coastguard (HMCG) as the Small Ship Safety Channel (UK only).

## Public Correspondence

Many channels were allocated for ship-to-shore telephone calls (link calls). Due to the popularity of mobile phones and satellite communications, many states, including the UK and France, have closed their coast radio stations for economic reasons. However, the service is still available in some European countries such as the Republic of Ireland.

Link calls were made using duplex channels. A number of them are now not used. Unfortunately, they cannot generally be used for inter-ship calls but HMCG uses a few for weather forecasts and navigational warnings.

## Procedure Words (Prowords)

Prowords might be described as those the professionals use. All are designed for easy international understanding and brevity. Not included are rambling pieces of chat such as: "I am signing off this channel now but will listen for any further communication from you. Have a good day!"

The Standard Marine Communication Phrases (SMCP) is published by the IMO (www.imo.org). Shown below are the words that candidates for the SRC examination need to know.

THIS IS – From a station whose name or call sign immediately follows.

OVER – The invitation to reply. "Over and out" is NEVER used.

OUT – This is said by each station at the end of working.

REQUEST RADIO CHECK – Please tell me the strength and clarity of my transmission.

I SAY AGAIN – I am repeating what I have just said (or a portion of it).

STATION CALLING – Used when a station receives a call which is intended for it but is uncertain of the identification of the calling station.

READ BACK – Please read back the message that I have just sent to you.

WRONG – Reply to a message that has just been 'read back' but is in error.

CORRECT – Reply to a message that has been read back for check.

CORRECTION – Spoken when a mistake has been made. The correct words or group follows.

RECEIVED – Your message has been received and understood.

WAIT – If a station is unable to accept traffic immediately, it will reply with the words "Wait x minutes".

I SPELL – I shall spell the next word or group.

ALL AFTER – Used after the prowords "Say again" to request the repetition of a portion of a list or message.

ALL BEFORE – Used after the prowords "Say again" to request the repetition of a portion of a list or message.

REPEAT – Used if any part of a message is considered important to need emphasising. Example: *My intended berth is Delta three zero – repeat – Delta three zero. Over.*

# ANNEXES

## Phonetic Alphabet & Figure Spelling Tables

### Phonetic Alphabet

Letter word pronounced as:

| | | |
|---|---|---|
| A | Alfa | AL FAH |
| B | Bravo | BRAH VOH |
| C | Charlie | CHAR LEE or SHAR LEE |
| D | Delta | DELL TAH |
| E | Echo | ECK OH |
| F | Foxtrot | FOKS TROT |
| G | Golf | GOLF |
| H | Hotel | HOH TELL |
| I | India | IN DEE AH |
| J | Juliet | JEW LEE ETT |
| K | Kilo | KEY LOH |
| L | Lima | LEE MAH |
| M | Mike | MIKE |
| N | November | NO VEM BER |
| O | Oscar | OSS CAH |
| P | Papa | PAH PAH |
| Q | Quebec | KEH BECK |
| R | Romeo | ROW ME OH |
| S | Sierra | SEE AIR RAH |
| T | Tango | TANG GO |
| U | Uniform | YOU NEE FORM or OO NEE FORM |
| V | Victor | VIK TAH |
| W | Whiskey | WISS KEY |
| X | X-ray | ECKS RAY |
| Y | Yankee | YANG KEY |
| Z | Zulu | ZOO LOO |

Note: The syllables to be emphasised are underlined.

# ANNEXES

## Phonetic Numerals

When numerals are transmitted by radiotelephone, the following rules for their pronunciation should be observed:

Numeral spoken as:

| | |
|---|---|
| 1 | UNA-WUN |
| 2 | BISSO-TOO |
| 3 | TERRA-TREE |
| 4 | KARTE-<u>FOW</u>-ER |
| 5 | PANTA-FIFE |
| 6 | SOXI-SIX |
| 7 | SETTE-<u>SEV</u>-EN |
| 8 | OKTO-AIT |
| 9 | NOVE-<u>NIN</u>-ER |
| 0 | NADA-ZERO |

Typically the number prefixes are dropped in day-to-day use.

Numerals should be transmitted digit by digit.

**RYA** Handy Guide to Marine Radio (inc. GMDSS)

# ANNEXES

## Distress Procedure – Card 1

The following procedure card should be displayed in full view of the VHF radio installation.

This Distress Procedure card is for vessels FITTED WITH DIGITAL SELECTIVE CALLING.

**Distress Procedure**

Name of Vessel ………......…………..…     MMSI ………………..………..…     Call sign …………….................……

**DISTRESS ALERTS** are to be made only when **IMMEDIATE ASSISTANCE IS REQUIRED**.

What you must do:

- Check that the main battery is switched on
- Switch on the VHF/DSC
- Open the cover to the RED Distress button
- Press the RED button once
- If time permits, select DISTRESS TYPE e.g. SINKING, FIRE etc.
- Press and hold the RED button down for five seconds
- Wait for 15 seconds then DEPRESS THE TRANSMIT BUTTON on the hand microphone
- Speaking SLOWLY and CLEARLY into the microphone SAY:

**MAYDAY, MAYDAY, MAYDAY**

**THIS IS** (Repeat name of vessel three times)

**CALL SIGN** and **MMSI**

**MAYDAY** (Name of vessel spoken once)

**CALL SIGN** and **MMSI**

**MY POSITION IS** (Latitude and longitude or True bearing and distance from a charted feature)

**NATURE OF DISTRESS** (e.g. sinking, on fire)

**I REQUIRE IMMEDIATE ASSISTANCE**

**NUMBER OF PERSONS ON BOARD and OTHER USEFUL INFORMATION**

**OVER**

- Release the transmit button and wait for an acknowledgement
- Keep listening on Channel 16 for instructions
- If an acknowledgement is not received repeat the voice Distress call and message

# ANNEXES

## Distress Procedure – Card 2

The following procedure card should be displayed in full view of the VHF radio installation.

This version is for vessels NOT FITTED WITH DIGITAL SELECTIVE CALLING.

### Distress Procedure

Name of Vessel ………......……....………..………..…    Call sign …………..............…................................

**DISTRESS CALLS** are to be made only when **IMMEDIATE ASSISTANCE IS REQUIRED.**

What you must do:

- Check that the main battery is switched on

- Switch on the VHF. Check Channel 16 25W is selected

- **DEPRESS THE TRANSMIT BUTTON** on the hand microphone

- Speaking SLOWLY and CLEARLY into the microphone SAY:

**MAYDAY, MAYDAY, MAYDAY**

**THIS IS** (Repeat name of vessel three times)

**CALL SIGN** (See above)

**MAYDAY AND CALL SIGN** (Name of vessel spoken once and call sign)

**MY POSITION IS** (Latitude and longitude or True bearing and distance from a charted feature)

**NATURE OF DISTRESS** (e.g. sinking, on fire)

**I REQUIRE IMMEDIATE ASSISTANCE**

**NUMBER OF PERSONS ON BOARD and OTHER USEFUL INFORMATION**

**OVER**

- Release the transmit button and wait for an acknowledgement

- Keep listening on Channel 16 for instructions

- If an acknowledgement is not received repeat the voice Distress call and message

# ANNEXES

## VHF Channel Allocation

| Channel Number | Transmitting freq. | | Intership Single freq. | Port ops | | Public correspondence | Notes |
|---|---|---|---|---|---|---|---|
| | Ship Station | Coast Station | | Single freq. | Two freq. | | |
| 01 | 156.050 | 160.650 | | Yes | Yes | Yes | |
| 02 | 156.100 | 160.700 | | Yes | Yes | Yes | |
| 03 | 156.150 | 160.750 | | Yes | Yes | Yes | |
| 04 | 156.200 | 160.800 | | Yes | Yes | Yes | |
| 05 | 156.250 | 160.850 | | Yes | Yes | Yes | |
| 06 | 156.300 | | Yes | | | | SHIP TO SHIP |
| 07 | 156.350 | 160.950 | | Yes | Yes | Yes | |
| 08 | 156.400 | | Yes | | | | SHIP TO SHIP |
| 09 | 156.450 | 156.450 | Yes | Yes | | | Used by pilots |
| 10 | 156.500 | 156.500 | Yes | Yes | | | Used by HM Coastguard |
| 11 | 156.550 | 156.550 | | Yes | | | Port operations |
| 12 | 156.600 | 156.600 | | Yes | | | Port operations |
| 13 | 156.650 | 156.650 | Yes | Yes | | | Bridge-to-bridge working |
| 14 | 156.700 | 156.700 | | Yes | | | Port operations |
| 15 | 156.750 | 156.750 | Yes | Yes | | | On-board working |
| **16** | **156.800** | **156.800** | **DISTRESS SAFETY AND CALLING** | | | | |
| 17 | 156.850 | 156.850 | Yes | Yes | | | On-board working |
| 18 | 156.900 | 161.500 | | Yes | Yes | Yes | |
| 19 | 156.950 | 161.550 | | Yes | Yes | Yes | |
| 20 | 157.000 | 161.600 | | Yes | Yes | Yes | |
| 21 | 157.050 | 161.650 | | Yes | Yes | Yes | |
| 22 | 157.100 | 161.700 | | Yes | Yes | Yes | |
| 23 | 157.150 | 161.750 | | Yes | Yes | Yes | |
| 24 | 157.200 | 161.800 | | Yes | Yes | Yes | |
| 25 | 157.250 | 161.850 | | Yes | Yes | Yes | |
| 26 | 157.300 | 161.900 | | Yes | Yes | Yes | |
| 27 | 157.350 | 161.950 | | | Yes | Yes | |
| 28 | 157.400 | 162.000 | | | Yes | Yes | |
| 60 | 156.025 | 160.625 | | Yes | Yes | Yes | |
| 61 | 156.075 | 160.675 | | Yes | Yes | Yes | |
| 62 | 156.125 | 160.725 | | Yes | Yes | Yes | HMCG MSI broadcasts |
| 63 | 156.175 | 160.775 | | Yes | Yes | Yes | |
| 64 | 156.225 | 160.825 | | Yes | Yes | Yes | |
| 65 | 156.275 | 160.875 | | Yes | Yes | Yes | |

# ANNEXES

| | | | | | | | |
|---|---|---|---|---|---|---|---|
| 66 | 156.325 | 160.925 | | Yes | Yes | Yes | |
| 67 | 156.375 | 156.375 | Yes | Yes | | | UK Small Ship Safety |
| 68 | 156.425 | 156.425 | | Yes | | | |
| 69 | 156.475 | 156.475 | Yes | Yes | | | Port Operations 70 |
| **70** | **156.525** | **156.525** | **NOT TO BE USED FOR VOICE COMMUNICATIONS** | | | | **Digital Selective Calling** |
| 71 | 156.575 | 156.575 | | Yes | | | |
| 72 | 156.625 | | Yes | | | | SHIP TO SHIP |
| 73 | 156.675 | 156.675 | Yes | Yes | | | Used by HM Coastguard |
| 74 | 156.725 | 156.725 | | Yes | | | |
| 75 | 156.775 | 156.775 | | Yes | | | Navigation communications 1w or geographical spacing |
| 76 | 156.825 | 156.825 | | Yes | | | |
| 77 | 156.875 | | Yes | | | | SHIP TO SHIP |
| 78 | 156.925 | 161.525 | | Yes | Yes | Yes | |
| 79 | 156.975 | 161.575 | | Yes | Yes | Yes | |
| 80 | 157.025 | 161.625 | | Yes | Yes | Yes | Marinas (UK only) |
| 81 | 157.075 | 161.675 | | Yes | Yes | Yes | |
| 82 | 157.125 | 161.725 | | Yes | Yes | Yes | |
| 83 | 157.175 | 161.775 | | Yes | Yes | Yes | |
| 84 | 157.225 | 161.825 | | Yes | Yes | Yes | |
| 85 | 157.275 | 161.875 | | Yes | Yes | Yes | |
| 86 | 157.325 | 161.925 | | Yes | Yes | Yes | |
| 87 | 157.375 | 157.375 | | Yes | | | |
| 88 | 157.425 | 157.425 | | Yes | | | |
| AIS 1 | 161.975 | 161.975 | | | | | A.I.S. |
| AIS 2 | 162.025 | 162.025 | | | | | A.I.S. |
| M1 (37) | 157.850 | 157.850 | | Yes | | | UK "private" channels dedicated to marinas, yacht clubs, and recreational craft |
| M2 | 161.425 | 161.425 | | Yes | | | |

Note: Many channels are shown as both single- and dual-frequency in this table. These channels may be operated as single-frequency channels subject to special arrangement between interested or affected administrations.

Channel 80 is a dual-frequency channel which is used in the UK for communication between marinas and vessels.

**No communication is possible between two vessels on a dual-frequency channel when using semi-duplex equt.**